The Lord Works in Mysterious Ways

Richard Little

authorHOUSE®

AuthorHouse™
1663 Liberty Drive
Bloomington, IN 47403
www.authorhouse.com
Phone: 1 (800) 839-8640

Published by AuthorHouse 04/09/2018

ISBN: 978-1-5462-3145-5 (sc)
ISBN: 978-1-5462-3144-8 (e)

Library of Congress Control Number: 2018902939

Print information available on the last page.

This book is printed on acid-free paper.

Chapter One

In The Beginning

Our story begins with the birth of a boy to a family in Eisleben, Germany in 1908. He was the second son of Anne Robelen Luddel and Harvey J. Luddel. The boys name was Richard and he had an older brother James. What makes this story significant is that son of a Jewish mother and a Lutheran father was that the Lord had given him a special gift that was realized later in his life. The boys grew up in this small German village south east of Berlin and took part in the activities of most children of the time. Anne was from a very large family and many of her brother and sisters had moved to the United States shortly before World War I. This will become very important later on in the story. Harvey was a piano and organ tuner and he had a brother who was the Pastor of the village Lutheran Church. The family made a modest living and lived in a small row home in the village.

The oldest son James graduated from school and was able to learn a trade of welding in a steel mill when they were very busy with the World War I effort. During the later part of World War I the younger son Richard was in high school and he was found to be very bright young man. In fact the German school system considered him gifted. He was able to skip two years of school and was the youngest person ever to graduate from high school at the age of 16.

By this time the war was over in Germany in 1918. Between the high war debt and high inflation the economy in Germany was very bad to say the least. After the World Wide Depression of 1929 It got even worse. It took a basket of Marks even to buy a loaf of bread. The Luddel family living with modest limited means did not have the finances to send a gifted child to college and it was felt that he was to young. James was now working part time in the local steel mill as a maintenance welder. Only emergency maintenance was being performed.

The school system notified the government of the unusual student and the government took over the further education of the young man. However the government would have total control of what was studied and what the degree program would be in. The student became a ward of the government and attended Berlin University taking Combustion Engineering (explosives), with a full math government scholarship. Upon completion of the degree program he was required to work for the government until the cost of the degree program was paid off as so directed by the government, but at least he had a job in a very bad economic times.

When the degree program was completed the recent graduate was required to work on a special top secret government project called the heavy water project on primarily a math and research. This was the early research of the German development of their new weapons program.

Because of the economy of the country was in such bad shape a group of thug's called brown shirts started stirring up the people, getting into government and blaming all the financial problems of the country on the Jews, which was anything but true. The truth of the mater is that conditions in the country were very bad so someone or group had to be at fault. They happened to be a convent escape goat. Establishments were being bombed and set fire, and Jews were being stoned to death. The country was turning to mob rule when a young radical and head of the brown shirts came to power, Adolf Hitler. His power slowly grew as conditions got worse, because people thought he had answers to the growing problem. Total respect for ones neighbor was breaking down.

Harvey Luddel had a brother who was a pastor in a local community Lutheran Church. One Sunday in the early 30's about 1934 he spoke out in a sermon on how wrong it was in the mistreatment of fellow Germans especially the Jewish members of the community. He was arrested on the steps of the church by the police shortly their after. After many hours of questing he was released with a warning to never preach on that subject again. The following Sunday his sermon was on his arrest and what had happened. He was arrested again and this time he disappeared.

Harvey Luddel and his family tried to diplomatically find out what happened. It was as if the powers to be in the community just swallowed him up and he was never heard of again. At this point the family got very concerned. If this could happen to a Christian Pastor on the steps of his own church how save was the rest of the family, especially Harvey's wife Anne who was a Jew. Everyone was very concerned about their safety and tried to come up with a plan on what to do next.

After much thought a plan started to develop. It was felt that the only place Anne would be save would be out of the country. This all had to kept very secret. No one must find out or they all would be arrested. The plan was to visit relatives in Austria. They had a cousin their who was about to have a birthday. The plan was for the family to visit the cousin in Austria and keep on going since the borders were still open in Austria. To go anywhere in or out of Germany you needed a travel pass. This was applied for. The members of the family withdrew what little savings they could without drawing suspicion to themselves. When they got the travel pass, they packed up their travel cloths in suit cases and boarded a train for Austria. Everything seamed to be going as planned until they stopped at the border by the police. Their travel paper work was checked as well as their personal identification paper work. They had a concern about the one government employee leaving the country. After assuring the police that they were only visiting family in Austria for a few days and would be back. The family thought this might happen and had purchased round trip train tickets. After showing the police the return tickets in a few days and again assured them they were only visiting family, they were allowed to go on.

The cousin was a son of Harvey's brother who had been arrested knew what had happened to his father and had contacted a local Lutheran Bishop who was an old friend. Feeling the house was being watched. The family fled at night with the help of the Lutheran Church over the border.

Passage had been arranged with false identification on an old tramp steam freighter to Great Britain.

When in Britain the necessary paper work was filed with the American Embassy for passage to the United States. To come to the United States at this time you needed a sponsor. Anne had a brother Frank Robelen who owned a music company in Wilmington, Delaware called The Robelen Piano Company. Frank Robelen agreed to be their sponsor, hire Harvey, and help the two sons find employment. While all the paper work was being processed they stayed in the home of some members of local Lutheran Church. Funds that they had brought along were running out so Frank help pay for their passage to the States. They arrived in New York, and after processing at Elis Island. Frank drove to New York and picked them up to take them to his home in Wilmington, Delaware.

Chapter Two

Home In The New World

Starting a new life in the United States was not easy. Harvey had a job working for his brother in law Frank, but the thought of starting all over again in his late 40's concerned him. The main reason for coming was the safety of his wife Anne who he loved very much. She definitely was not safe in what was becoming the new Germany. Now she was safe with several sisters and brothers who had come to the United States years earlier and had become citizens. She had a sister Else and a brother Frank who lived in Wilmington, and a sister Ella and a brother John who lived in Claymont, Delaware. Harvey could not forget the home he had built and he and Anne had furnished. All this the business he had cultivated and the friends he had made was all left behind. It wasn't a whole lot but it was his and Anne's and now it was gone. Harvey enjoyed working for Frank and he was treated well, but his heart was in what was left behind. Harvey grew listless, was not eating well, and become sick. He had accomplished what he set out to do and that was ensure his wife was safe. The doctors said the stress of everything he was going through was too much for him and he passed away.

The two sons now had the responsibility of taking care of their mother. James, an experienced welder got a job at Atlantic Refining located on the Delaware River between Wilmington and Philadelphia. Richard found out that his degree in Combustion Engineering did not help much. Richard started taking courses in electrical engineering and got a job as a yard master on the Baltimore and Ohio Railroad in the Elsmere Yard out side of Wilmington, Delaware. As mentioned the two brothers supported their mother after the loss of their father who lived in a row home in Wilmington. By the end of the 1930's, Richard had his electrical engineering degree and the whole family had become American Citizens. The most difficult part was overcoming the language barrier. Richard upon obtaining his second degree obtained a job with Honeywell Control Systems as a field engineer, left the railroad position, which he did not especially like, but provided a needed income.

The two boys still living at home and taking care of their mother starting to do some dating. James met a young lady that worked in a tavern near the refinery on the Delaware River where he worked. After dating Lillian for several years they got married and moved to a suburb of Philadelphia not to far of a drive from the refinery. Richard met a young nurse on a blind date that a fellow engineer at Honeywell had set up with the nurses older sister. The blind date must have gone well because Richard kept on dating Thelma.

Now Thelma was the next to the youngest of four

children of a family that had come over to this country from Great Britain after World War I. Thelma's father was a Scottish Cabinet Maker who did beautiful wood work, and her mother had worked in a British hand grenade factory during the first world war. As I mentioned they had four children, three girls and a boy, Robert who was the youngest.

After dating for quite a while Thelma got engaged to be married. Thelma's mother Elizabeth was totally against her daughter marring a person of German decent and refused to go to the wedding. Thelma and Richard still got married despite her mother's objection and purchased a row home in German Town, a suburb of Philadelphia. Despite Elizabeth's objection, Anne and she were swapping recipes a few weeks later and became good friends.

Now Anne was making some changes in her own life with her sons leaving home. It was the Lutheran Church that helped the family get out of Germany and her deceased husband Harvey was Lutheran. Anne started attending the Lutheran Church and met a man about the same age who had lost his wife to cancer. They started dating and Anne became a member of the Lutheran Church, much to some of her Jewish family's dismay. The man Anne was dating was a freight engineer on the Philadelphia, Baltimore, and Washington division of the Pennsylvania Railroad. His name was William and he had five grown children. William was nearing retirement on the railroad after working on the railroad for over fifty years. William was a Mason and Anne became very active in the Eastern Star. They got married and went on a honey moon at Niagara Falls. They took the Nickel Plate Road to New York. The Nickel Plate used steam locomotives not used on the Pennsylvania. So

William took the trip in the cab of the locomotive much to Anne dismay, but she understood this railroad man and still loved him. William treated Anne's family just like they was his own and vise-versa. William retired from the railroad and they bought a home at the corner of Concord Road and West Chester Pike, east of West Chester, Pa. The area is all built up now, but then is wasn't and William use to go out every morning walking with a basket on his arm and pick wild berries and nuts and bring them home. Anne would make breads and cookies and pies from them or William made home brew wine from them. At the end of the thirties everything was going relatively well despite the depression.

Thelma and Richard had moved into their row home in German Town. Richard was working as a control engineer for Honeywell Controls and Thelma was working as a registered nurse in Wilmington, Delaware when Thelma became pregnant. Nine months later Thelma gave birth to Phyllis, who died at the Memorial Hospital of Wilmington Delaware two days later. Thelma and Richard took it very hard. Thelma wanted to move from the area and get a fresh start. Richard built them a new home in King of Prussia, PA. The home was a cape cod style brick home located across the street from where the largest mall in Pennsylvania is now. Then it was a pig farm. The couple moved into their new cape cod home about the same time war started to engulf Europe.

Chapter Three

United States Enters World War II

About a year after they moved into their new cape cod home Thelma became pregnant again. Seven months later a boy was born in Jefferson Hospital, Philadelphia, but not without complications. The two and a half pound baby was not expected to live, but Thelma had made up her mind that she was not going to lose another baby. She kept the baby warm with hot water bottles in the crib and feed him every two hours and he started to gain weight. Because of the early birth the babies sinus's and nasal passages were not fully developed and the baby could only breathe through its mouth. At this point the baby was to frail to be operated on. Thelma and Richard decided they wanted to show the babies heritage in its name. The First name would be Richard after his father and king Richard of England and Scotland. The middle name would be Robelen, Which was the Jewish family name of Anne, Richards mother.

The baby was only about six months old when December

7th of 1941 happened and the United States entered the war. In early 1942 all immigrants from Germany, Italy, and Japan would be getting a visit from the state department and you were required to be home at the time of the visit. If they were not home they would be subject to arrest. Thelma, Richard, and the baby were home as requested when the state department visited. Their first question was! What brings you to the United States? Richard's mother Anne was Jewish and it was no longer safe in Germany. That was very understandable. Their next question was! Who did you work for in Germany? Richard's response was that he had gone through college in Germany on a government scholarship and was required to work for the government until it was paid off. That caused a bit of a stir in the visitors when they asked what he did for the government! Richard's answer really caused them to take notice. He said he was a scientist and mathematician on the heavy water project, which was the German development of the Atomic Bomb. At that they said they would be back in two weeks and again they were required to be there.

In the afternoon two weeks later the visitors from the State Department were back with an offer that could not be refused. Richard was to work on a special project, later to be known as the Manhattan Project, for the government. If he volunteered Thelma, he, and the baby would be moved to Tennessee at government expense. If he did not volunteer he would be drafted for the project without his family being moved. Thelma spoke up and said he would volunteer, but with one stipulation, and that was the last name would be changed from Luddel to Little. After some discussion the government decided that was a resemble request. The family was relocated to a suburb of Knoxville, Tennessee at government expense and Richard started working at Oakridge. Upon successful completion of the project the family would be moved back to Pennsylvania if that is what they desired.

Now let me tell you a funny little story that is true, but does not sound real. Richard was given the opportunity to look for a place to live between Knoxville and Oakridge before they moved. When Richard signed the motel register. He signed it Richard Luddel, King of Prussia, PA. He found a secluded ranch home in the woods, which is where they relocated to. When it came time to pay the motel bill their was no charge. With Richard's accent the clerk thought he was the King of Prussia and said it was a pleasure to have such an honored guest. Richard tried to explain, but to no avail.

As I mentioned the family relocated to Tennessee. Thelma my mother did not especially like Tennessee. We had a nice home in the woods with over a hundred trees. Dad had put up a cloths line to dry our cloths after they were washed. Lizards use to run up and down the cloths line, which mom found very unsettling. Dad had built me a sand box in the back yard to play in. One afternoon a deer came running across the back yard. I went running for mom for I had seen a horse with horns. The heat in Tennessee was from burning soft coal and that use to turn the inside of the house a din gee gray that had to be scrubbed or repainted every year. In 1944 Richard and Thelma had another baby boy. This one came in the normal nine months without a problem. Thelma and Richard again wanted to show the family heritage in the name. The first name would be Solomon, after the King of Israel, the middle name was Murray which was moms Scottish Clan madden name.

In 1945 the project had been a success. Two atomic bombs had brought an end to the war after being dropped on Japan. Dad had to make a very difficult decision. The decision that had to be made was to receive a sizable promotion and stay in Tennessee or move back to Pennsylvania where we would be near the rest of the family. Dad was pondering this decision when something else happened to effect our community in Tennessee. The Tennessee Valley Authority, TVA, which was a very large power project had hired a young engineer from Drexel University in Philadelphia, PA. His last name was Goldstein. He had put a deposit on a home next to where we lived. The lady across the street had started circulating a petition to keep the undesirable Jews from moving. This was before the law changed and if everyone on the street signed petition it would block the sale. Well dad was the last signature needed because they thought he would surely sign. I was helping dad in his vegetable garden weed when he was approached. Dad read the petition and asked a question. If Jesus Christ put a deposit on a house on the street would she circulate a petition? Her response was of course not, that is different. Dad's response was! How is that different he was a Jew. I think these people have suffered enough I am not signing the petition. The husband to the lady with petition was a member of town council and the community started to make things very difficult for our family. Dad could not believe people could be so cruel and predigest. We decided to move back to Pennsylvania where people were more open minded.

Chapter Four

Back to Pennsylvania

We relocated back to Pennsylvania in 1946. By that time dad had two sons. Dad was told, the way to keep boys out of trouble was to have a small farm. Mom and Dad bought a small farm from a road contractor who had built a five car garage/barn with a large loft for equipment storage and repair. It had a very large vineyard and a area for a large vegetable garden.

The house had a summer kitchen for canning and a inside kitchen for cooking in the winter. It had one bath, an add on to the summer kitchen roof with its own heating system. It was located about twenty miles east if West Chester in East Goshen Township. The small farm was just a little south of West Chester Pike in a little community called Mill Town. Philadelphia was thirty miles to the east. When we moved here Solomon was two and I was five. Because of my slow start in life I looked the same age as Solomon, but I was old enough for a Dr. Kauffman to fix my sinus and nasal problem that I was born with. Dr. Kauffman fixed the problem, but I was sick a lot growing up. I started school a years behind everyone else because I was small and rather sickly. The local public school had outside bathroom facilities for grades one and two in East Goshen. So I started school at a private Quaker School called Westtown Friends School for two years. I started the third grade at a public school. A two room school house in East Goshen at the intersection of 352 and Paoli Pike. Two grades were in each room with a teacher for each room. The school bus use to pick up the teachers at the trolley stop along the Red Arrow Line that ran from Philadelphia to West Chester on our way to school. The school building is now a church. When I started the third grade the third grade already knew how to write so I had some catching up to do. My penmanship suffered as a result, but it did not cause me to be pushed back a year, which is what I was afraid of.

Going to seventh grade in a large county Junior / Senior High School was an eye opening experience to say the least. Let me explain. In the two room township school you had all your classes taught by the same teacher for two years in the same room. At West Chester Joint Junior / Senior High School each class was in a different room with a different teacher in a large building it was easy to get lost in. Another thing that I noticed but not nearly as important to me as getting lost was the township school was all white. At West Chester it was pretty much 50 / 50. When I started the seventh grade I had a home room teacher by the name of Mr. Anderson, who I also had for geography. Mr. Anderson took me kind of under his wing and showed me where all my classes were and how to get there on time. Mr. Anderson was a black gentleman, but that did not matter to me as far as I was concerned he saved my life. I appreciated Mr.

Anderson's help so much that I asked mom and dad if I could invite them to dinner. Mom and dad never asked if he was white or not and to me it did not matter. He helped me through a very difficult time. The Anderson's did not drive so I met Mr. and Mrs. Anderson at the Milltown Trolley Station at the bottom of the hill and we walked up Locust Street hill to our small farm. Mom had prepared a very nice dinner and everything went very well. I walked the Anderson's back to the trolley station and walked back home after they left for West Chester. When I got home all hell broke loose and I had no idea that my mother was that predigest against black people. Needless to say I did not invite any other of my teachers to the house for dinner. Solomon did not have the same problem because by the time he finished the sixth grade the township school had gotten a lot bigger with a lot more teachers. It was like a small version of the high school and their for not nearly as intimidating. All through junior and senior high school I had a lot of colds and sinus infections. About once or twice a year for a couple of years I had to go back to Jefferson Hospital to have my sinuses flushed out with salt water, which was not pleasant but it kept the infections under control for months afterward. By senior high I had pretty much out grown the problem.

Solomon and I spent most of our childhood growing up in Milltown. We lived there for about fourteen years. Other than having very strict parents life was pretty uneventful, Let me explain. When Solomon and I were both in high school we were required to make to honor roll every marking period or we were considered dumb and were confined to our room to study after our chores were completed until the next marking period. No play or extra activities just study. I was sick a lot in my younger years so I spent a lot of time in my room studying. As I mentioned we had a small farm in Milltown. We grew all our own food. Solomon and I cultivated, planted, weeded, and harvested all by hand. We had a one furrow plow and cultivator with a large wheel and steering handles. Solomon and I took turns pulling or steering. Mom canned everything that was grown. Dad went together with a neighbor and bought a steer and had it butchered. Mom had a large flower garden and that was maintained by Solomon and I. Solomon and I did not get an allowance. If we wanted money we had to go out and earn it. When I was old enough in the summer I use to work as a migrant worker in an orchard and get paid so much a basket to pick. Mom got a discount on fruit as a result and she use to can a couple of bushels at a time. Our small farm had a small apple orchard of about eight trees until Hurricane Hazel took them all down. Mom made apple sauce until that happened. I must say some good pies came from those trees. In March of 1958 we had three feet of wet snow and lost power for about ten days. We still had water for drinking, cooking, and washing because the old farm house had a two cycle pump with a large wheel. Dad put a stool in front of the wheel and Solomon and I took turns walking on the wheel to build up pressure for water. Dad had the farm to keep us out of trouble and busy. Well I would say that was very successful.

Mom was raised a very conservative Scottish Presbyterian. I was baptized Presbyterian before we moved to Tennessee. Between Oakridge and Knoxville there were only Baptist Churches. So I attended Baptist Sunday School.

Mom joined me for church after Sunday School. Because I started attending Baptist Sunday School in Tennessee we continued going to a Baptist Sunday School and Church after we moved back to Pennsylvania located on West Chester Pike. Mom felt it was very important that we attend regularly. Even when it snowed and we could not get out.

Solomon and I would walk down the Trolley tracks to church a couple of miles down the road. The Pastor lived in Milltown so it was never a problem getting home. Solomon and I went to church their until we left home for college or the military.

In the 50's several members of the community came to see my father. We had the largest barn/garage structure in the community and they felt their was a need for a fire company, since there was not any in East Goshen Township. An used Hale Fire Truck was purchased and placed in one of the large bays of the structure. The fire company was called Goshen Fire Company, and became one of the largest most active companies in the area. It was the only fire company east of West Chester and was located on our property for several years. Dad was one of the charter members. They eventually built their own fire house about five miles west of where we lived. They had a large field next to the fire house where they had a fair every year to raise money for the fire company. It became one of the largest country fairs in eastern Pennsylvania. The whole family helped out fair week to raise money for the fire company.

Chapter Five

The 1960's Brought Difficult Times

The first thing that happened was that my fathers step father died after a long illness and blood circulation problems. He lost a leg do to the circulation problem which made him bed ridden and things rapidly went down hill after that. He had been a very active person. Worked on the Pennsylvania Railroad for over fifty years, walked miles a day, and had a large vegetable garden. He could not handle the inactivity and basically gave up. Now Anne was getting up in years and she did not drive. She did not have to, whenever she had to go some where we only lived about ten or so miles away we would pick her up and take her. Every week we took her grocery shopping. Her house was only a couple of miles out of West Chester on the West Chester Pike. My brother and I helped out with the lighting and scenery for stage productions at the high school. When ever we stayed after school to work we would tell mom we will call you from grandmother's house. Anne always had something good out of the oven to eat before we called mom for a ride. Dads answer to his mother living alone was adding an apartment above the barn/garage. Dad drew up a plan and applied for a building permit. Before he got an answer dad was called away on business by the government.

My father became well known with his engineering ability. I mentioned earlier of his help at Oakridge, Tennessee. Well after we moved back to Pennsylvania dad worked for Hagan Chemicals and Controls. While with them he help design the nuclear plant at Peach Bottom, PA., the merchant marine ship Savanna (an experimental nuclear ship that did not last long), and the USS Enterprise. He worked on controls of conventional power plants as well, but was a recommended consultant for nuclear power by the government. In this case it was to the French government for six or so months. Dad traveled a lot, mom was use to it, so this was not unusual, just longer than normal. My brother and I were in high school in West Chester and between that and the farm we were kept very busy. I was a high school Junior in 1959 and had to decide where I had to go to college after I graduated from high school. After much soul searching and prayer I applied and was accepted at North Eastern Institute of Christian Education. I wanted to be a history teacher or a preacher. I wasn't sure which so I was to start by studying Christian Education. I was pretty proud of what I had accomplished and thought dad would be proud when he got home. Mom did not have a problem with my decision. During my junior year of high school I started having increasing problems with my sinuses.

About half way through my junior year dad came home from France. The first thing that happened was he found that his building permit had been turned down. Dad went in orbit. After all he had done for the community how could they do such a thing. Being upset he put the farm up for sale. If he could not do what he wanted he would move else where. Dad sold the farm in a short time especially since it had a price tag of only $10,000 dollars. To give you an idea of this low price ten years later it sold for over $100,000 dollars. We relocated to Westtown Township where dad had large split level home with a apartment for his mother upstairs. She had her own bed room, sitting room, and bath. Anne came down stairs for meals. Between the money for the farm and what dad had earned from the French trip he paid cash for the house. It all happened so quick East Goshen Township did not have a chance to get back to him, because they decided to OK the building permit. They did not want the Little's to move from the township, but it was to little to late.

The next big thing that happened that sent dad in orbit was my decision to go to North Eastern Institute of Christian Education. I was breaking a Jewish tradition by not doing what my father did for an occupation. By not doing that I was breaking the Ten Commandments by showing disrespect to my father. About the same time I started having a lot of sinus trouble, which started getting infections in them a lot because they were not draining properly. What happened was my facial bone structure changed do to adolescence. My parents took me to a ear, nose, and throat doctor in West Chester. He said the surgery that was done by Dr. Kauffman at Jefferson Hospital in Philadelphia when I was about five had collapsed and I would need more surgery to reopen the sinuses. He could do the surgery. The E.N.T doctor performed the surgery at a West Chester Hospital. When I got home from the hospital mom insisted on giving me a milk shake. I tried to tell her I could no drink it, with a very messed up vocal ability, but she insisted. So I drank it and it came out my nose and all over everything. She was horrified and called the doctor. He had mom bring me into the office and he examined the surgery. I had a lot of difficulty talking and could only drink with my fingers holding my nose closed. My father's response to this mess was that the Lord was punishing me for disobeying my father's wishes. I was crushed to say the least. I could not attend school with this problem. So I had to repeat my eleventh year of high school, which was a blessing I did not realize at the time. It was obvious I was not going to North Eastern to be a teacher or a pastor. I found it very difficult to talk at all and to be understood, the E.N.T. doctor made a plate without teeth for my mouth, that helped some with my speech, but I still had squeaks and whistles when I talked and liquids still came out my nose, which was very messy and annoying. By summer it was realized that the hole in the roof of my mouth was not going to close without more surgery. I went back into West Chester Hospital for more surgery. The E.N.T doctor cut all the tissue from one side of my mouth roof and flopped it over the hole and pinned it on the other side. I was in a lot of pain for weeks, but it worked. I was very limited on what I could eat or drink for a while, but it did not come out my nose any more. It changed my voice which caused me to undergo a lot of kidding when I went back to school, because I sounded like Elmer Fud in the cartoons, but at least I could talk. I thought the dream I had of what I wanted to do with my life in the future was gone. What I found however is that the Lord does work in mysterious ways. I will explain later.

In the fall of 1960 I started back to school. The year before I had kept up with most of my studies even though I was home. So this year was a lot easier and I was able to stay on the honor roll most of the year. I had a full load of classes and had almost enough credits to graduate except for English. This started me thinking. I started school late because of health reasons and I had to repeat the eleventh year because of health reasons. Now I was finally going to graduate from high school in 1961, but I was going to be 20 years old and my brother three years younger was only a year behind me. I had to get a jump on my education to earn a decent living. I still had some trouble speaking and my father objected to what I thought I wanted to do. I had a hobby of model railroading and electronics. If I pursued this my father probably would not object. By this time Solomon and I had a newspaper route and I had been saving my half of the profits. I needed some other jobs beside this to earn some money. I wasn't going to ask dad for any help financially. I started working part time washing dishes and working as a short order cook at a pharmacy in a strip mall not to far from the high school, and helping the builder of our house with odd jobs on the weekends. By time I started my last year of high school I was excepted at a night trade school on 69th street, Philadelphia. I had saved enough to pay the entrance fees and my first semester. Every spare minute was spent studying. I use to get to high school early on the bus. I used to sit on the floor outside my home room studying. On the trolley back and forth to Philadelphia I was studying. During the study halls of which I had many because I did not need to many credits to graduate I studied or worked on scenery for school plays. I graduated from West Chester High School in May of 1961 as a honor roll student and had finished my first year of trade school on the deans list. I continued going to trade school without any breaks. Working on a farm in the early morning milking cows, going to class after that and working in the pharmacy after that. I got home studied grabbed a few hours sleep and did it again the next day. I dated a good looking Irish girl once after fixing her stereo system, she had beautiful red hair. Mom found out and did not approve. When I got home from working at the pharmacy I found all my belongings on the front porch. Mom told me either I stopped seeing that Irish girl up the street or I would no longer be living under this roof. Moving out at midnight was not a good option, so I stopped seeing the girl up the street. By late summer 1962 I had my associate engineering degree in electronics. I held a first class communications federal license, one of the youngest to do so in Pennsylvania, and finished my degree program on the dean's list. To go for my BS degree I would have to college full time and that would cost a lot more money. I started looking around, but everyone wanted some experience beside my education. As I said asking my father for money was not a option. By now I had an additional problem. If I was not attending a college full time I was going to get drafted.

Chapter Six

Starting a New Career

One afternoon in early fall I got and idea. I told my parents I had to pickup some paper work at the tax office in the basement of the West Chester Post Office, which I did, but I also enlisted in the U.S. Navy. They were in need of young people with my educational background. They promised to pay for the rest of my college and I would be working in electronics getting the experience I needed. I enlisted in the U.S. Navy. I did not tell my parents because of the strong difference of opinion with my father and mom wanted me to stay at home. I wanted to make my own way. I did not tell my parents until the night before I left for boot camp. Mom went in orbit as expected, but dad did not have anything to say. Mom tried to get dad to call some of his political friends, but dad said it was to late. I left for boot camp at the Great Lakes Naval Station the next morning. I found it physical more demanding than I had anticipated, but I made it. Upon graduating from boot camp I thought I would spend the next couple of weeks working in the chow hall while awaiting orders. That did not happen, at 2:00 am in the morning I was woken up because I had orders to a ship out of Norfolk, Virginia because of my electronic background and the Navy was short of technicians. I flew to Norfolk on a two engine prop aircraft which was the military version of a DC3. I prayed I would get their ok, because when I looked out the window you could see a liquid streaming out the engine and blowing off into the air while the engine rivets walked in and out. This did not give me a warm fuzzy feeling. A Navy bus picked me up at the air strip and took me too the destroyer pier where I boarded the USS Bearss, DD654. Before 8:00 in the morning we were headed out to sea. I was part of the first division. I was asked if I had any cooking experience and since I had one of my duties was cooking in the chiefs mess. There is only about six chiefs on a destroyer so the job was pretty easy. My other duties was working with the deck force performing ships maintenance and helping the electronics technicians with repairs as a stricker. I did not realize it at first, but this old Flectcher Class World War II destroyer was part of a blockade of Cuba during the missile crises in the fall of 1962. We patrolled the South Atlantic until the blockade was over and then headed for Baltimore, Maryland. We were to have an open house of one of the blockade ships for the residents of Baltimore. We neared Baltimore on a Friday evening. A member of the port authority boarded us and guided us to dock at the end of Baltimore Street, I was helmsmen at the time, what an experience. I had duty on Saturday, but had Sunday off.

We did not have chaplain on board so when we were in port a list of church services were listed on the quarterdeck. I wrote down some addresses, put on my dress uniform, put my bible under my arm and headed for church Sunday morning early. I was headed up Baltimore Street when I heard foot steps behind me and someone call hay sailor do you have any money. I started to walk faster and the steps behind me went faster when I heard a second voice call hay sailor do you have any money. I started running and whatever was behind me started running. I scaled a high rod iron fence ran through a cemetery and in the back door of a church. It was a German Lutheran Church and the whole service was in German. I did not understand much of it at all, but I did not care I felt safe. The congregation was very friendly after the service. I looked outside! What ever was chasing me was gone. I saw the high fence and figured I only went over it with the Lords help. I did not here the bad reputation of Baltimore Street until some time later. I made my way back to the ship without any further incident. Monday morning early we were back out to sea on patrol along with a new destroyer escort ship(DE) out of Norfolk on a shake down cruise. The DE developed some compass troubles and guided on us until they got a handle on it and then headed back to Norfolk. We were headed for Bermuda. We were in sight of the island coast when our orders were changed because of a hurricane. The storm passed us by and it was a bad one. We followed the storm back to Norfolk. I was helmsman for part of the journey. I wondered if we were a submarine or a destroyer. We were taking waves between the stacks. We took quite a pounding. We developed a leak in the bow filling the chain locker and food storage locker full of sea water. The next compartment back was my living compartment. It took all our pumps running to keep us afloat. The number one gun mount all the way forward looked like it was sitting on the ocean. We could not come into Norfolk because of the storm, so had to weigh anker next to the cruiser USS Newport News, which was relatively new at this point. We looked like we had gone through the war. I had orders for the Navies ET "A" School at this point and left the USS Bearss. I had made seaman (E3). I was off to school after a short levee at home and I would never see this old destroyer again, although it brings back many memories.

Chapter Seven

Great Lakes
ET"A" School

Since I had made seaman and all the others in the class were seaman apprentices I was put in charge of a barracks. The Navies Electronics "A" School, Great Lakes had all frame, wood, barracks insulated with straw built as temporary housing during the war. They were two story H shaped buildings with four dorms. Each dorm had two picnic tables in the middle for studying. Each table had a large coffee can with water in it for smoking. This was the only area you were allowed to smoke. In 1963 it was mandatory that everyone go to church on Sunday. I had a barracks of primarily New York, Irish Catholic's so I marched them to mass on Sunday morning. I attended a Protestant service afterwards. The chapels at the Great Lakes were impressive structures. I did not write home to mom about any of this because she was very anti-Catholic. I looked at it as a learning experience. The mass in the 60's was in Latin, but the prayer book was written in Latin on one page and English on the next so you could follow along. I soon realized that Catholics believed in pretty much the same things I did as a Protestant. So this proved to be a good learning experience that proved to be helpful later in life. The Irish and I developed a good relationship and we helped each other out with our studies and played games such as tennis together.

On non-duty weekends my mother mentioned I had an aunt in Park Ridge, on my fathers side of the family. They had fixed up the basement as an apartment for a son who had gone to medical school. I was there on off duty weekends and helped out with some maintenance issues around the house. I attended church with them on Sunday mornings and then took the train back to the base. I graduated first in my class from the Navies, Electronics "A" School at the Great Lakes, Naval Station, but not without some incidents.

The men in the barracks were getting letters from their girlfriends back home. I thought and then I membered their was this blond with pretty blue eyes on my news paper route. Her name was Kathryn Heal and we had also graduated the same year from high school. I started writing and she started writing back. After high school she started working at F.W. Woolworths, in charge of the pet department. She knew my mom and mentioned to mom one afternoon in Woolworths that she received a letter from me. My next letter from mom she asked what church Kate attended. This proved not to be a problem since Kate and her family attended Holy Trinity Episcopal Church in West Chester, The Episcopal Church is the same as the Church of England so mom did not have a problem.

The first ten weeks of class was all algebra. I was cruising along with all 100's on the tests. We got a unit exam every two weeks. As I said I was cruising along with a high average when I went to take a unit exam for about week twenty when some officers and chiefs took me in a separate room to take the exam. If I dropped a pencil they picked it up and inspected it. To have consistently have such a high average they told me I must be riding a horse or cheating. They wanted to know how I was doing it. I told them I was not cheating and if they had checked my service record they would have seen I had two years of electronics in college and I had been on the dean's list. I got a 87.5 on this exam and a apology from the school staff. The last ten weeks of Navy E.T. School was on equipment, which I found more difficult, my final average when I graduated was 89.49. With such a high average I was told I would get duty of my choice. I found when this is offered it is not necessarily true. I had asked for any destroyer on the east coast. I got Navy Communications Station (NAU) Sabana Seca, Puerto Rico after a short leave at home.

Before I left the Great Lakes Naval Station one other incident happened. As I mentioned before I was in charge of one of these frame barracks built as temporary barracks insulated with straw during World War II, but still in use. Since most of us in the barracks were nearing the end of our training a new sailor was assigned to my barracks. I woke everybody up in the morning by going around inside of a trash can with a coke bottle and hollering rivalry all hands on deck. I made my rounds and this new sailor did not get up. In fact he started smoking in his rack. I told him this was not allowed and it was a serious safety hazard because of the frame barracks which could burn down in minutes with a great loss of life. There was a designated smoking area with butt cans on the picnic tables in the middle of the barracks. I told him to get up before I came back from my round. I came back from my next round around the barracks and he was still in his rack still smoking. I told him to get up and go to the smoking area or I would have to put him on report. He told me to go to hell. I reluctantly put him on report, and he went before the training center officers. He said he and his friends would beat me up at the train station when we graduated. Several of my Irish friends who had cars on the base took me to a different train station to avoid a problem. Upon leaving the Great Lakes Naval Station I had two weeks leave at home. I will never forget the day I got home, it was the same day President Kennedy was killed. After my two weeks leave, most of which I spent most of at Kate's on the other side of the hill, much to my mother's dismay. I reported to the Philadelphia Naval Yard where I picked up my orders to the radio station and my tickets.

Chapter Eight

Nav. Comm. Sta. Puerto Rico NAU

I flew to Puerto Rico and arrived at the San Juan Airport late evening wearing my dress blue wool uniform. When I got off the plain I thought someone had poured fifty gallons of water over me I was soaked through due to the very high humidity and temperature. I was to report to the Naval Station on arriving on the island. I had no idea where that was so I flagged a taxi. The taxi driver saw I was new to the island and charged me fifty dollars to go about a mile. That was the last time that was allowed to happen. I reported to the Naval Station and they said I was to be stationed at the radio station about twenty five miles into the mountains and I could take a navy bus out there in the morning. I spent the night at the Naval Station. While I was at the Philadelphia Naval Yard I took the third class electronic petty officers test. Since I just graduated first in my class from the Navy's ET "A" School. I found the test pretty easy. Shortly after I was stationed at the radio station

I was notified I made ETN3 in the first increment. I was put in charge of inventorying a electronics ware house until my top secret clearance came through. I found out that I was taking inventory because the Communication Officer LT. Navy(division officer) was being replaced by a LT. Hollman because Mr. Nave was being transferred. The new officer had to sign for all the equipment in the ware house.

Now the ware house did not have a restroom(head), that still meant that you still needed a means to wipe ones self if you had to go. You are probably thinking why not go back to the communications center. Well the ware house was about a mile from the center and off the base in a bunker cut in the side of a mountain built for mutation storage during WWII. In fact from a tree on top of the bunker you could see the whole base. LT. Hollman was a rather young officer who got his commission as a result of a NROTC program where he went to college. That saying he went strictly by the book. When I turned in a requisition for toilet paper, it was disapproved because the ware house did not have a head, so I had to result to stealing some from the center. After the inventory was complete, Mr. Hollman went to the ware house with me for a day to spot check the inventory. While he was checking the inventory he asked me where the head was? I reminded him we did not have one. He asked what we did if we had to go? I grabbed a piece of the roughest packing paper I could find, and told him we just went into the jungle to relive our self. An amazing thing happened after that. The next day the ware house was issued a case of toilet paper. Mr. Hollman learned that some things are not so cut and dried, and in time we became good friends. I am not going into to much detail on the two and a half years

I was stationed at the Sabanna Seca Naval Radio Station. I am just going to give you some of the high points.

As a Petty Officer I had to have Shore Patrol duties once a month, which was done by a rotation of Petty Officers in the communications division made up of radioman and electronic technicians. On my second month in the rotation I noticed we picked a lot of the same young people for minor officious, mainly graffiti on buildings. The following Monday a group of us asked for a meeting of the Commander of the Base. We had our meeting with the Commander, and we told him we had repeatedly picked up the same young people for minor officious. These are not bad young people. He asked if we had any suggestions. Our reply was yes sir. He asked what that might be. These young people are getting into trouble because there is not anything for them to do. We would like to start a boy scout troop and a Sunday School, to keep them busy and to teach them right from wrong. He said this ways beyond his expertise, but he would set up a meeting with the chaplains at the Naval Station in San Juan. How it is important that I add a little note here. The radio station had a chapel but no chaplain. The Navy had a policy that to receive a chaplain you had to have a active congregation for two years and we did not have that at the present time. The Naval Station was thirty miles of dirt road away, which we traveled to meet with the chaplains. They consisted of three Catholic Priests and a Rabbi, no Protestant Pastor. They lessoned to what we had to say and thought it was a good idea. We stated we wanted a non-demonational Sunday School Material since we did not know the religious make up of the radio station. The chaplains set up a meeting with the Puerto Rico Virgin

Islands Scout Commencer with us and Sabanna Seca Troop 170 was started. We were one of three English speaking troops of 125 on the island. From here to the end of the book I am going to give just the high points and not as much detail, because it was quite a long process and I do not want to bore you with details. We made an announcement in the daily plain of the day about the starting of a boy scout troop and a Sunday School on Sunday Mornings at 0900 with refreshments. The troop took off first with about two dozen boys and quite a few men from the barrack and housing area which wanted to help. This was a added benefit that initial planning petty officers did not plan on. The navy donated an old spare underground bunker for us to meet in. Some of the boys had been in scouting before and had progressed in rank, so we formed two patrols, rattle snack and eagle. The bunker was at the edge of the base so it was convenient for the boys to get to. The navy had power run to the bunker for us, so the boys and the volunteers started renovating the bunker. Many of the volunteers had trades and became merit badge cancellers in the process. The supply officer notified me of unclaimed materials after they sat for a couple of weeks and our volunteers were pretty good at scrounging. This operation was a little shady at times but worked out. We got the bunker about half renovated when base officers wanted it for an Officers Club. This was a minor setback, but the navy gave us another bunker and promised we would not lose this one. This bunker was off the base in the jungle about a quarter of a mile away. This posed some initial problems and the bunker was not in very good shape. The boys, our leadership, and volunteers took this challenge in stride and we made it work out. Oh I did not tell you of our leadership. The Scoutmaster was a Chief Hospital Corpsman, another second class petty officer (Ron Miller) and I were Assistant Scoutmasters. We used kerosene lamps in the bunker initially, until the Sea Bee's ran telephone poles and electric out to the bunker. Then renovation started with much vigor. We cleared out the brush and bushes from around the bunker so we could play some games such as capture the flag. The scoutmaster and some of the corpsman who worked for him trained the boys in first aid. The Base Security Force Marines lead by Gunny Sargent George Washington trained the boys in marksmanship and how to handle and clean a rifle. I must admit the Gunny was a lot easier on the boys when they were on the marine range than he was with sailors on the range. Sailors had to qualify on the marine range every six months with both the rifle and the pistol, which was no easy task.

We needed tents for camping. This posed somewhat of a problem. Ron, the chief, or I could not figure out a way for the navy to supply tents, when I had to do calibration of some microwave communication equipment the navy had at an army reserve training base called Fort Buchanan, named after a Pennsylvania President. The army had a warehouse right across the street from the building where I had to calibrate the equipment. On the loading dock of the warehouse was a pile of tent halves, poles, and pegs. They sat out there on the loading dock the whole week I was calibrating the equipment across the street. I was afraid someone would take the tent halves, so I took them for safe keeping. They were in the back of my jeep when I left the Fort and waved through the security gate on way back to the radio station. We had tents for the boys to go camping.

I thought I was caught one weekend when a navy officer visiting the camp sight asked what the U.S.A. stood for on the tents. I said United States of America. He accepted my answer. We were out camping at least one weekend a month. Base security checked on our wellbeing when they made their rounds for our own safety. One weekend we camped next to a grove of dead bamboo thinking that would be good kindling wood for start a camp fire after dark. We often had young piece crop people helping us. Many of which played guitars so we often sat around a camp fire and roasted marshmallows and sang songs. That afternoon I dove into my tent and I came flying out one end of the tent and a baby boa snake came out the other end. We checked the other tents and found two more. We did not know where they were coming from until that evening when we chopped into the grove of dead bamboo and found a very large boa snake. It lunged at us, but we still had a machete in our hands and swung taking off his head. Needles to say we moved the tents shortly their after. A mongoose must have taken away the remains of the snake during the night, because it was gone by morning.

In the summer of 1964 troop 170 of Sabana Seca Naval Radio Station went on a camporee of the Puerto Rico Virgin Islands Council. Ron, the chief, and I got Navy Orders cut to go on a camporee on the south side of the island for a week with 125 troops of the council. We got help of the piece crop, since we were one of only three English speaking troops in the council. The Navy supplied a bus for the trip. It was on a beautiful white sand beach called Leaquo Beach not too far from the city of Ponce on the south side of the island. It was a computation of scouting skills between patrols and our two made us feel proud. The Eagle and Rattle Snack patrols came out first and second in the computation, and we only had one incident happen on the trip. You can tell boys to stop running around they may trip, but they do not lesson until it happens. One rather hefty young man tripped on a tent peg and fell. His arm swelled up. We did not know if it was broke or not, it was very sensitive. The closest place for military assistance was over a hundred miles away so that was not an option. The closest hospital was in Ponce. We got a ride over to the hospital. The smell in the hospital was terrible and there was only one nurse for the whole floor. The doctor and x-ray technician were on call. We had the x-ray technician called in. while we were waiting I had to go to the restroom It smelled so bad and the flies were so bad I felt I did not have to go that bad. The latrine at the camp site was cleaner. While we were waiting for the technician an ambulance came in with a machete accident. It was too serious to be handled there. The ambulance was sent to San Juan. The student technician came and took the x-ray but he did not know how to read them. The Medical Corpsman Chief was with us and he could read the x-ray. Thank God it was only a bad sprain. The chief put it in a sling and we went back to the camp site.

As I said it was a beautiful white sand beach with a lot of cocoa nut palm trees so we had to be careful where we pitched our tents, because of fallowing coconuts. What I found out during the night that crabs made their home in sand and wanted to join you in your sleeping bag which is not a good experience. A week away from Naval Radio Station we were glad to head back.

I have been going on about my scouting experience and

there was a second program that started after our meeting with the Naval Station Chaplains, that is a Sunday School program started at the base chapel. A box of Sunday School Materials was shipped to the Naval Radio Station from Cook Publications. Our class met on Sunday mornings a 0900. We started with a class of nine which grew to a class of over a dozen, which included some adults that wanted to see a regular church service started. That is when I realized the Lord works in mysterious ways. My father would not let me go to a Christian College, but here I was doing the Lords work. It was truly an example of a door being closed to me and the Lord opening a window. As our numbers grew over the next six months we thought we were ready for the next step. The same group of petty officers that met with the base commander asked to meet with him again. We brought him up to date on our progress, which he was happy to hear, and told us the incidence of vandalism had stopped on the base. He set up another meeting for us to meet with the Naval Station Chaplains. We brought the Chaplains up to date on what was transpiring on the base, which they were happy to hear. We asked them if a regular church could be started on Sunday morning since some of the adults in the Sunday School Class had expressed a desire for that to happen. They went over the Navy policy for base chaplain with us, which was that a service had to be in existence for two years before a chaplain got assigned to the base. They said however that none of us were ordained they were willing to send a chaplain out once a month for communion, but we had to take turns on Sunday Mornings holding a church service. They would provide the bulletins, hymnals, and would help with guidance with the sermon. A petty officer who did not have the duty that weekend would man the pulpit. There was three of us, so we made up what was then called the Naval Radio Station Chaplains Committee. It is interesting to note that after navy service one of these became a Methodist Pastor in New England, one became a used car salesmen in the Midwest, and one became an engineer in Pennsylvania. We started our church services, which was a little crude at first because we did not have a piano or organ and had to sing Hymans by our memory and we were not use to following the program outlines provided by the chaplains, but things got better with time and we got a guitar instrument help from someone who starting coming from the barracks. A Chaplain came out from the Naval Station once a month to hold a communion. We had Sunday School after the church service with donuts, coffee, and juice. After two years our little chapel service was assigned a Protestant Chaplain, a Lt. Robert Edwards. To my surprise after my transfer to the active naval reserves in 1966 I received a letter of appreciation, which was to be added to my service record. I included the letter with at the end of the book. I sang in the church choir, but only because I was only one of a few sailors that were sober on a Sunday Morning. By the time I left the base the church had about one hundred person attendance.

While stationed at the Naval Radio Station I finished my B.S. Degree program. Mr. Hollman was very understanding and the navy work schedule was worked around my classes. I also made second class petty officer. Shortly after I made second class I was made crew supervisor of a night shift maintenance crew, which helped a lot with my college classes, but I functioned on very little sleep. The Base

Commander was told that the communications center did not meet the requirements of a top secret communications center, and that our communications could be picked up outside the base in the clear. The navy was given one year to clear up the problem or it would be shut down by the defense department. The only ones allowed to work inside the facility were the eighteen electronic technicians, they were divided into two crews of nine. This is when I was made crew supervisor of night shift. We worked from 1800 at night to 0600 in the morning six days a week. We had off Sundays for Church. All the cables were replaced, the walls and ceilings were replaced with special shielded material. This is when we discovered a major asbestos problem, but in the 60's we did not know it was dangerous. The two teams of technicians got the job done in nine months, which pleased both the navy and the defense department.

In October of 1965 during morning muster and inspection Chief Addison, 1st Class Petty Officer Murphy, and I were selected to go to Mr. Holman's Office. When we went into Mr. Holman's office we were told we had volunteered for a special mission. An uprising had occurred in the Dominican Republic we were to be temporarily assigned to the United States Embassy to hook up emergency communications between the embassy and hear to be forwarded to Washington D.C. Rebels had taken over the telephone exchange and embassy communications was no longer reliable. President Johnson had sent in the USS Boxer with a company of Marines to secure American Property. We flew by helicopter to the Dominican Republic Airport where we were met by a jeep and taken to the U.S. Embassy. The chief and I went right to work checking out an old cable that had gone from the embassy to a hanger at the airport. The chief and I found a couple of wires that were not shorted or open that might be used as key lines. We hooked up a piece of crypto equipment and a teletype in the basement of the embassy. We left Murphy in the basement and the chief and I went out to the airport hangar to connect up a transceiver to the key line. Amazing enough it worked. All that was left to do was to hook up an antenna to communicate to the radio station. Chief Addison was going to go up the pole to connect the antenna, but I said no he was married with children. I was the only single person of the three so it should be I. Besides the Marines had cleared the area we should not have problem. The marines put a sharp shooter at the base of the pole just in case and I went up the pole with a cable and an antenna. I got the antenna connected in a drizzle rain when the sun decided to come out and so did a Cuban Regular Army sniper that was on a hanger roof behind a front over hang. He got of one shot and the marine sharp shooter took him off the roof. The marine called up to see if I was alright. I said I was only stung by a bee, which is what I thought it was until on my way back down I felt something wet and it was me bleeding. The communications link worked ok. The U.S. Marines discovered three warehouses of Russian and Chinese Arms, and Cuban propaganda. So was it a civil war which is what the newspapers called it. A M.A.S.H hospital was set up in El Marro Castle, which was built with English slaves hundreds of years ago, when Spain was a major power is where I was sent. It was a cold damp place and I got one infection after another. I went from 135 pounds down to 97 before I was released from the hospital. I am glad my injury was not serious.

I was only back to the Naval Radio Station a few months to finish the micro-wave installation before I finished my enlistment. That reminds me I did not say much about the micro-wave installation I was part of. Shortly after I made third class petty officer I was sent to micro-wave school at Fort Allen. I went to school about two weeks and graduated high man in my class, only to find out when I got back to my base that a Chief Bishop was my boss. The chief went to micro-wave school at the same time skip most of the classes in favor of the golf course and got the lowest grade in the class, but he was a chief so he was my boss. We did not get along to well technically and he liked to hit the bottle. Most of the time his thinking was scrambled, but I learned to work around it and tried to avoid the chief, which was not too hard since he was usually at the club drinking. What was bad he wrote up my quarterly marks. My technical marks were very good but my military marks were as low as the chief could make them without having to explain.

The last month I was at the Naval Radio Station I was called into Mr. Hollmans office. He said according to my records you have only stood one monthly Naval District Inspection since you have been here. You were always on duty somewhere else. I do not know how you did that, but if you are not at the next one I am going to find out. I was at the next inspection. If the truth be told when I stood Naval District Inspection the first time. The Commandant of the naval district showed up two hours late. Marines were dropping like flies in there wool uniforms in the hot sun. The Admiral showed up in a spaghetti stained uniform and had the nerve to inspect looking like that, so for the next two years I wade it a point to be somewhere else when the inspection was held. The district inspections were always held on a Saturday and the micro-wave maintenance crew took turns with on call duty on weekends. I just arranged to have the on call duty on inspection weekends and managed to get a service call the night before an inspection.

In December of 1965 I got transferred to the Charlestown, South Carolina Naval Base for separation from the active navy and to the reserves. I flew there from Ramey Air Force base on the north side of Puerto Rico, which was one of the bases I used cover for micro-wave maintenance. I was not treated to well at the Charlestown Naval Base because I was from the north in other words a yankee and these people were still fighting the civil war. I was a second class petty officer with over four years in the navy sweeping parking lots and had shore patrol every other night down in the slum bar section of the city, while southern seaman were in nice warm offices doing paper work. After several weeks of this I went to the petty officers club to drone my sowers where I met a second class corpsman from Wisconsin. He asked how long I had been hear and I said three weeks and he said why so long. I said I was just waiting for my separation physical, but my paper work was always bottom of the list because I was a Yankee. He said my records would be over in sickbay in the morning. Two days later I was standing my last shore patrol, because I had my plain tickets back to Pennsylvania. The southern third class yeoman asked how I accomplished that, I just said luck. My last shore patrol went well until the end of the watch. At the end of the patrol we would meet at the enlisted man's club, which was off the base. After last call when the club was closing a patty wagon would take us back to the base. This night proved to be different. There were about four shore patrol petty officer's waiting at the bar. Last call had been made, and the band was playing there last song, when the rotating mirrored ball in the ceiling shined on a metal object at one of the tables. It was a gun! The shore patrol officers jumped on this gentleman as the gun went off and the shot went into the ceiling. The bartender called the police before I called the shore patrol headquarters and have the officer of the watch come with the patty wagon. The Charlestown Chief arrived before the patty wagon and asked who was in charge. I looked and I was the senior petty officer there. I said I was and he said I might of known it would be a damn Yankee.The Duty Officer came in the patty wagon and took the sailor into custody.

Chapter Nine

Home

I flew out of Charlestown on Eastern Airlines at about 10:00 am. I was expected to be at Philadelphia Airport in the late afternoon. I was to be met at the Airport by Kate, who I was engaged to by this time, and my mother. We had a stop in North Carolina to pick up some more passengers. However part of the wing came off when we landed. We were told we could not take off because of minor technical difficulties. Kate and mom who were waiting for me in Philadelphia Airport from 3:00 pm on were told the same thing. Not until another plane arrived from Philadelphia and we were all transferred to it did we find out what really happened. I finally arrived at Philadelphia Airport at 11:00 pm in the evening. Kate and mom could hardly recognize me because I had lost so much weight in the M.A.S.H. hospital. The smallest waist for a navy uniform is a 28 inch waist and I was down to a 26. I had to where suspenders under my dress jumper to keep my 13 button trousers up. I was so glad to see them that we missed a turn while talking on the way home, but we finally made it. I was home and Christmas was only a few days away.

It was a great Christmas to be home with mom, dad, and grandma, who lived with my parents in like her own little apartment up stairs, but joined them for meals. I went to church with Kate, since I could not go back to church I was attending before I went into the navy. Oh! I forgot to tell you that story. While I was in the M.A.S.H. hospital recovering. Chaplain Edwards brought me a letter from the Baptist Church Pastor where I once attended and he had read the engagement announcement that was in the local paper. It stated I was engaged to a Kathryn Ann Heal and we would be marrying in April of 1966 at Holy Trinity Episcopal Church. Since I was not marrying a member of the Baptist Church I was going to hell. I let Chaplain Edwards read the letter, He was sorry he brought me the letter. I told him there was nothing to be sorry for it was a Baptist Pastor who burnt the bridge. I went to church with Kate and her mother. Later on before we were married we also attended marriage classes from Rev. Anthony of Holy Trinity.

Kate's older brother Jim married a nurse by the name of Rhoda at Holy Trinity in January. Jim and Rhoda also attended marriage classes with Rev. Anthony before they were married. As part of the class you had to take a marriage test. Kate and I took the test and we failed it badly. Rev. Anthony wanted us to attend a marriage seminar in Philadelphia. Rev. Anthony got the test results after we were married, and he had married us. He called Kate's mother and she told him we were on our honeymoon.

Kate and I had gotten engaged on Easter of 1965. I got

the rings from the Caribe Diamond Company, through the Navy Exchange. That was I did not have to pay any taxes. The engagement ring was ¾ of a caret, and I mailed it with an Easter egg to Kate. I ensured it for about for about four hundred dollars and sent that paper work to mom. The package I sent Kate was stopped at the Federal Post Office in Philadelphia and they would not forward it to West Chester. I do not know why, unless it was the insurance.

Kate found out on Good Friday, which was a very busy day a Woolworths where she worked in the pet department. Mr. Hagan her boss let her go to Philadelphia to pick up the package. So her mother, my mother, and Kate drove to Philadelphia to get the package at the Federal Post Office. The building was old and hot and not air-conditioned. The Easter egg had melted on to the ring. I had wrapped it and rewrapped it, and then wrapped again. When they all got to the post office in Philadelphia all they had to open the well wrapped package was a finger nail file, so it took a while to accomplish the job, and being very anxious to see what was inside did not help the situation. Kate wore the ring to work the next day. Mr. Hagan asked to see it. It was a little loose so he told her to have a guard put on it. He did not want her losing it in a fish tank.

It was a busy few months for us. We had to make up a guest list, send out announcements, find an apartment, get a physical, get a wedding license, and schedule a church service. I had gotten a job at Harrow Servo Controls on Westtown Road at the edge of the town of West Chester. I was in charge of calibration of instruments. They made servo motors for N.A.S.A. and the airline industry. I had a salary of $100.00 a week, which in 1966 I thought was a lot of money. Kate and I found an apartment on Union Street, just a few blocks in back of the church where we would be married. It was in a row house and consisted of a bed room, a living room a very large kitchen and a bath room on the first floor for only $80.00 a month. The landlords were the Hoffman's, who lived next door. Kate had purchased a used car with the help of her father. It was a Dodge with an automatic transmission. I had driver training in high school, but did not get my Pennsylvania Driver's License until I was home from the navy. I had a federal license in Puerto Rico where I was stationed, which was not valued in the states, but gave me driving experience on a manual military jeep. We purchased a few pieces of furniture from Kauffman Furniture in West Chester with some money I had sent home while in the navy. The salesman was a high school classmate who gave us a good deal. The furniture would be delivered a day or two before the wedding. Everything was falling in place. We selected the wedding party which included Kate's sister Eileen as maid of honor and my brother Solomon as best man. We were married April 16, 1966 in the evening. We were to have a candle light wedding, but they forgot to light the candles. The reception was in the basement of the church. We went on a honeymoon in the Pocono's at Birchwood. We were gone a week. All the couples at Birchwood were married that same weekend. The staff at Birchwood had a lot of fun activities for us. We had a good time before we headed back to West Chester. We had a stack of mail when we got back including a letter from the Department of the Navy. When I came of active duty in Charlestown I thought I was in the inactive for the next eighteen months of my six year enlistment. While I was stationed in Puerto Rico the Secretary of Defense, Mr. McNamara made some changes with enlistments do to the War in Vietnam. If you got your degree or if you had over a year of service schools you had to stay active or at least stay in the active reserves for the full six years. I had gotten my degree and I had over a year of service schools so I had to serve in the active reserves in Folsom, Naval Reserve Training Center near Chester, PA. I had to report right after I got back from our Honeymoon, three days a week for three hours a night. Needless to say Kate did not like pressing white uniforms. The first six months was not bad, I was teaching electronics to radioman, sonar man, and radar man who now had to have some knowledge of electronics for advancement in rate. The next year was terrible, for some unknown reason the navy opened up the reserves to anyone off the street. I ended up with a class of fifty, which was a way to big, of thugs off the streets of Chester who were only trying to avoid the draft and Vietnam. Carried nothing about the navy and did not want to hear what I had to say. I was espoused to teach them "The Uniform Code of Military Justice, "which some of them was going to need. After the first hour I was horse. When class started again I gave them a choice of seating quietly and taking notes or spend the rest of the time marching on the drill field. They chose the drill field. I figured if I could not instill something in their heads maybe I could instill something in their feet. That is how the next year went until I finished my enlistment.

Chapter Ten

Five Years Later

It now five years later. Kate and I are no longer living on Union Street. We moved from their about a year after we were married. We found a home we could afford under the GI bill in Merriweather Farms a development of California Style Ranchers on Paoli Pike not far from where Kate worked. We bought it for $16,000.00 with a 4.5% mortgage, we could afford with a little pinching. It looked pretty empty with the little bit of furniture we had, but it was all ours. It was a three bedroom house so we had room to grow a family. The car port had been made into a spare room which is where I put my model railroad. My father helped me put a fence around the back yard so we could get a dog. We got a mutt from the Human Society. A small honey color retriever mix with a brown nose and yellow eyes. Kate working at the pet department at Woolworth's gave us an opportunity to have a lot of pets. Hamsters, fish, and even a parrot for awhile.

Shortly after we moved I got a much better job with the company who made the crypto equipment I worked on in the navy. Burroughs Corporation, I got a much better salary with better medical benefits working as a test engineer. My father was not happy I was working for Burroughs, but he helped me find a second car cheap, which would help me get back and forth to Paoli, Pennsylvania, which is where the new job was located. I was hired by the military division of Burroughs on a new top secret all solid state computer called Illiac IV, being built for N.A.S.A. Little did I know that during the five years of working on this project that the engineers working on this very large system would find ourselves pictured in National Geographic. It had 64 parallel processors, a control unit so big it took a sliding double garage door to get access to the backplane, and a laser memory. While I was working on Illiac I found out that the military keeps close tabs on people with crypto top secret clearances. The spy ship USS Pueblo was taken by the North Korean's, The crew had destroyed the manuals for the crypto equipment, but the equipment was taken intact. I was one of the few people that had worked on that equipment and knew how to get it to work without a manual. I got a call one afternoon at Burroughs by the defense department and asked not to leave the country. My response ways that I did not have any intent in leaving the country.

Kate and went to Holy Trinity Church with her mother initially. We could walk to church from where we lived on Union Street. We did not feel overly comfortable here because it was so large and the only one we knew was her mother. We were invited to visit a small country church in Unionville by one of Kate's fish customers, which we did. We liked it so much and the Pastor and his wife were so friendly and made us feel wanted. We started attending regularly, and eventually became members at Unionville Presbyterian Church.

After we were married for a couple of years we decided to start a family. Kate was not using any form of birth control, so after many months of trying we decided to see a specialist. We found out that my sperm was almost dead do the way we installed micro-wave links in the navy. To install a link we eye balled it with binoculars and a compass from the tower behind the dish. Then we powered up the link at both ends, which was in the low end of the x-ray band, climbed the tower again with a meter connected to the micro-wave transceiver. We straddled the feed horn and adjusted the dish with a couple of wrenches for a peak on the meter not realizing we were x-raying ourselves at the same time. It mentioned this was a possibility in the manuals, but we did not think about it, and this was the easiest way to bring up a link. I guess a couple of years of installing micro-wave links this way had a cumulative effect. Kate and I tried adapting in both Pennsylvania and Delaware. After two years of going to interviews and tests we were turned down in Pennsylvania, because they felt we could not love an adapted child as much as one of our own. Kate's grandfather had been a state senator so we thought we had some political pull in Delaware. Well they answered in a short time with a letter, which stated that they thought we had a good case in Pennsylvania, but we were not residents of Delaware so there for were denied. Kate and I were crushed. We had been taken temperature charts to find the best time and nothing seemed to work. Finally we decided to get away from it all and go to the mountains. My father's brother Jim had a cabin in the Grand Cannon of Pennsylvania, north of

Williamsport. We spent a week at the cabin. Before we left for the mountains, Kate was getting ready in the bed room, I got down on my knees and prayed in the dining room for a miracle to happen. Well guess what it happened Kate was pregnant. Some say it was the slope of the mountain. I don't, I think it was that prayer before we headed for the mountains. As I said before the Lord works in mysterious ways. Mark Richard Little was born March 1, 1971. He was a ten month baby that got stuck in the birth cannel so Kate had him C section. I am getting ahead of myself again. In December of 1967 my father died from blood cancer probably do to what he worked on during the war in Tennessee. Everyone on that project died of the same thing, but the government says that is only a coincidence. Kate's father was very happy she was pregnant, but he had a heart attack walking across the manufacturing area and died where he worked at Scott Paper in Chester the month before Kate was do. He had a physical the day before and they said he was ok. He so much wanted to see Kate's little one. Kate stopped working when she was pregnant because she was sick so much and by then I was making enough as a test engineer, working nights that she did not have to work for us to make ends meet. Mark ways a little over a year old when we starting finishing up on Illiac IV computer. I was interviewed for a position to go with the system to N.A.S.A. Aims Research Center in California. I said I could not go do to the recent passing of my father and father in law. They told me if there was not another government project to go on I would most likely be laid off. It became somewhat of a joke while we were running the exceptenance tests if you were called into the manager's office on a Wednesday for a cup of coffee you were laid off. If not you were good until the following Wednesday. My Wednesday eventually happened and I was laid off. Personal at the facility did not try to find you an opening in another division. When I got home that morning I starting calling other divisions. I contacted a Mr. Adams who had hired me initially only now he was a chief engineer with the small systems group in Downingtown, PA. He had an opening for a person to design power supplies. I said I had not designed a power supply since college, but I was willing to give it a go. The layoff was changed to a transfer. I was told I would be designing power supplies for six months, which lasted for two years before I got back to logic again. The good part of this is that I had spent the last three years on night shift and this test engineer's job was on day shift. Kate and I went out celebrating. How we did not know that her having Mark solved her problem. We thought it would take as long for a second baby as it did for the first. Well we were wrong. Nine months after our celebrating we had Holly Ann Little. There was nineteen months between them, which worked out very well. Holly was due on Christmas day. We knew she was going to be C section because Mark was. The good Jewish OB Kate had asked if she would like to be home for Christmas. She said that would be nice so Holly was born the thirteenth of December. We had a three bed room house so it worked out well, at least for a while. At two years old we started potty training Mark without much luck. Well Holly started going to the potty at eighteen months. When she started going to the potty, Mark decided his sister was not going to do something he was not willing to do so he started going to the potty also. Problem solved no more diapers.

They were two complete opposites. Mark had us up every two hours to be feed, and Holly slept all night at an early age. When Mark started walking he ran everywhere and ran into things. We were making regular trips to the emergency room at the local hospital. We were afraid we were going to be arrested for child abuse we were at the hospital so often. Mark finally grew out of it then but he was a very active boy.

The dog "Honey" we had went blind at about fourteen years old and started snapping at the children. We were afraid they were going to get bit. That would not be a good thing so we had to get rid of her. When Mark was about five we went to register him for school. We lived in West Goshen Township and it had an elementary school about two miles from the house near where Kate use to work on Paoli Pike. When I called the school the said Mark would be going to school at the elementary school on Gay Street in West Chester going right by the West Goshen elementary school. I felt this was wrong and I said so. I was told we did not have a choice. I said I did so we sold the house for over twenty thousand more than we paid for it and moved to Downingtown area in West Bradford Township. We put a deposit on a brick rancher on Hilltop Road, which was just west of Downingtown. It was about half the distance from where I worked and it was a much shorter drive from where Kate and I were going to church in Unionville. What we did not know was the single mother who lived in the house with several children had problems, so the quality of the house went downhill between when we put down our deposit and when we had closing on the house. In fact when we looked at it after closing it was a total mess. I wondered why we got it at a low prices and it was about to be sold at a sheriffs sale.

It had about an acre of property which had a lot of broken glass and the grass had not been cut in weeks. Some of the test engineers I worked with volunteered to help me clean up the outside. We picked up all the broken bottles and we came to the conclusion that there must have been one huge party before they left. There was marijuana growing in what used to be a vegetable garden. I took a cycle to that and put it in a trash bag. The trash man did not know he hauled away a fortune. Kate and I cleaned up the large basement, which even had a dead dog in it. I scrubbed the large kitchen floor several times before it became decent. After about a week of work we were finally ready to move in. Some friends from church helped us move from West Goshen to West Bradford Township, which took us from the West Chester School System which had bussing to solve its integration problem to the Downingtown School System which did not. There was already a good mixture of white and black throughout the Downingtown School System so it did not have the problem West Chester had. Kate and I got even more active in church in Unionville. We started teaching Sunday school and even sang in the choir for a while, since we were now living closer. The children liked going to West Bradford eliminatory very much. Kate and I got involved in Cub Scouts through the school. Mark advanced very well in the Cub Scouts and went on to the Boy Scouts by joining Troop 52 in Marshallton, Pennsylvania. A small town between Unionville and Downingtown. The sponsor of the troop was the Methodist Church in town. I started getting involved in scouting with Mark and became assistant scout master after I attending some adult training. Mark advanced to Eagle Scout and we were quite proud of him.

An English setter mix starting to show up at our door to play with the kids. We were rather leery of a strange dog although we feed and watered it. It ate well and acted like it was hungry. It was very friendly and was without a collar. We put an ad in the paper to see if someone claimed it, and someone did. They came to the door and accused us of stealing the dog. He gave us his name and address, took the dog, but acted very rude about the whole thing. The next day the dog came back shaking all over. We called his owner and he came back over in his pickup truck. Accused us of luring the dog away, took him and latterly through him in the back of the pickup. We called the S.P.C.A. and told them of what happened and gave them the name and address of the dog's owner. A short time later the owner of the dog came back and told us it was our dog. The S.P.C.A. told him he did not deserve a dog. We called him Spike took him to the vet to get all his shots and to check him out to see if he was healthy. Mark and Holly could do anything with that dog. Holly even dressed him in baby clothes and pushed him up and down the street in a baby carriage. Spike was a fun member of the family. Next door was a pure papered English Setter by the name of Samantha. Samantha was kept in a yard with a six foot high cyclone fence, which was in between the two yards. One afternoon while I was at work Kate was in the back yard with Spike, Mark, and Holly when Samantha came out in her back yard. She was in heat and went up and down the fence wiggling her backend at Spike. Well it was more than Spike could take. He went up that cyclone fence just like it was a ladder and nailed Samantha. Mark and Holly got a sex education that day. Samantha's owner came outside turned a hose on them and tried to pull them apart. Samantha's owner threatened to sue us for what Spike had done. We tried to explain that it was instigated by Samantha, but our relationship with our neighbors went downhill after that. In fact things got so bad we sold the house and moved to a very small community called Romansville. It was a rancher on a pie shaped lot across the street from a dairy farm owned by the Supple Family, who we went to church with. Mark had made Eagle Scout about this time with Boy Scout Troop 52, which we were both very active in. Mark also started at Downingtown High School, at which he started taking computer repair at vocational technical school. Romansville was a small village at a cross roads with four pie shaped pieces of property. It had a dairy farm, a general store, a gas station, and a Methodist Church. Oh and our house. We had a very large lot of just a little over an acre of ground. It was closer to Unionville Church than where we had lived. Which was a plus since we were all very active in church at Unionville. Kate and I were Sunday School Teachers and I was on the board of elders at the church. Holly was very active in the youth group at the church and was very involved in its activities. We liked this house and its location very much. We were thinking this would be a nice place to eventually retire. I put a rail fence around the property and lined a portion with mesh in the back yard to keep spike from going out in the street. I started planting fruit trees with the idea that I could have a fruit stand to sell fruit after I retired. We had a full basement which I divided in half. Half for the railroad and half for Kate to work on ceramics, she started to work on in her spare time. Mark got a job at the general store after school to start saving money for a car. Everything was going great I was still active in the boy scouts and Kate Holly and I were very active in church. Holly finished grade school and started going to Downingtown High School in the gifted students program. She was also became a very active soccer player in the township soccer program and ran cross country for Downingtown High School. The C.E.O. of Burroughs tries to make Burroughs bigger than I.B.M. through accusations' including a forcible takeover of Sperry Univac. The C.E.O. put the company nine billion dollars in debt. The merger with Sperry formed the Company Unisys in 1985.

Kate started having jaw bone problems after a botched surgery for TMJ in West Chester. The surgeon said Kate's jaw bone needed surgery that was beyond him. There was a surgeon in Wisconsin, and another one I California. Kate and I drove to Wisconsin via her Aunt and Uncles home in Crystal Lake, Illinois. We saw a Dr. Duran Ryan who we were very happy with. He felt he could help her, which proved to be a good choice with what was about to happen with Unisys.

Kate, I and the children were very happy in our home in Romansville. With mergers changes happen. Burroughs was the biggest employer in Chester County under Unisys it became the smallest with the closing of about six plants in Chester County, mostly in Downingtown but also the old Burroughs Military Division Headquarters in Paoli, and Great Valley Labs. It was soon realized that if I wanted to stay employed we were going to have to make some changes. The Tredyffrin facility where I was working at the time was to become an engineering management facility only. No manufacturing was to be done there. If I wanted a job with Unisys I was going to have to transfer. I got job offers from a central repair facility in Holland, OH and a manufacturing facility in Minneapolis, MN. I had job interviews in both locations. I took Kate with me to see the area of the country when I went for the interviews. I had over twenty years with the company at this point and if I wanted to stay with them I was going to have to take one of these offers if I wanted to stay with the company. Kate and I and the children really did not want to move but we had to for me to stay employed. We still had family in PA so that became the controlling factor. From MN it would take two days to get back to PA and it was much colder. From Holland, Ohio we could make it back in one day if we had to. So I took the job in Holland, Ohio. Unisys took over the sale of the house in Romansville and we moved to Ohio Christmas week of 1987 with the two children a dog a car and a truck. We got the children enrolled in Anthony Wayne High School. This was a good fit for Holly, who was in a gifted students program in PA. They had the same program in Ohio and even used the same books. This was a perfect fit for Holly, but Mark was a different story. Mark was taking a computer repair course at vocational technical school.

Chapter Eleven

Our Move to Ohio
To Stay Employed

In December of 1987 over Christmas Holiday we moved to Holland, Ohio. Kate and I after a long discussion figured the Ohio job was the best bet even though we really did not want to move. We still had family in Pennsylvania and we could make it back to PA in one day. The other location would take two days of travel one way. We were moving Mark in his junior year of high so I became public enemy number one. What made matters worse, he was taking computer repair at Vocational Technical School in Pennsylvania as I stated. The Anthony Wayne High School were Mark and Holly would be attending did not have anything close to what Mark was taking, so he had to take college prep. The new school worked out well for Holly. They had the same gifted student program as she was taking in Pennsylvania and even used the same books. For Holly it worked out well, but not nearly as well for Mark which I felt bad about.

Unisys bought the house in Pennsylvania and paid for

our move to Ohio. I still had a job as a Senior Quality Assurance Engineer working at their central repair center responsible for field reliability. I investigated assemblies that had high failure rates in the field and tried to solve the problem. All in all it was pretty interesting work, but entailed long hours. I was at work early talking to facilities in Europe and late talking to facilities on the west coast. I did not get paid extra for the long hours it was considered part of the job. I was so busy in my little world that I did not realize as Unisys phased out the old Pennsylvania products they were also phasing out the Pennsylvania people.

We bought an acre of corn field from a farmer that was right across from Oak Openings Metro Park. We enjoyed hiking the trails in the park. The park had several ponds that was fed by a creek that crossed the field below were we purchased our acre. Holly enjoyed running in the park and was sometimes accumpted by deer which ran along with her. Holly ran on the Anthony Wayne cross country and track team so running in the park was good practice. Mark graduated from Anthony Wayne High School and started going to a Owens Community College, not to far from where we lived. He worked part time as a co-op at Unisys, which proved to be good experience because he realized he liked mechanical engineering better than electrical. Mark bought a car before we moved from Pennsylvania, a twenty year old cougar, which resembled a ford mustang with flip up lights. It was red with a black vinyl top. We had it shipped to Ohio and I let Mark use the garage as a piece offering for moving when the house was built. We started to get settled in good and about the time Holly graduated from Anthony Wayne High School I was given the choice of early retirement or layoff. Holly graduated one of the top ten in her class and had colleges competing for her with scholarships. Holly was runner up in getting into the Naval Academy. The scholarships kept growing between Rutgers University and Alma Presbyterian College. The deciding factor was the percentage of women on the campus, because both institutions came up with about the same money in scholarships. The Rutgers campus was about 20% women while Alma was pretty much 50 – 50. Holly felt uncomfortable being part of a minority so she went to Alma, which was rated only second in the country in chemistry, which is what she wanted to major in.

Things were going pretty good when Unisys gave me a choice of early retirement or layoff. Well you really can not do either with two children in college. I took early retirement and we sold the house and moved to a rented house in Grand Rapids, Ohio. It was a two story house with a basement, but only the first floor was heated. I poured and fired ceramics in the basement, which Kate worked on in the very large kitchen. I got a part time job teaching at Owens Community College in Findlay, Ohio. Kate's Ceramic business, the pension, and my teaching part time kept us afloat until college expenses jumped and then I needed additional income. At this point I had to leave Owens and start working as a contract engineer. One of the contracts I had was with Monroe Auto Equipment, they had a contract with Ford to develop a variable suspension system on the Ford Explorer, which they were just coming out with. I help develop the circuit card for the suspension system. It worked so well that Ford called Monroe and asked if they were hiring me full time. Monroe Auto Equipment hired me, which gave Kate and I medical insurance again, which we had not have since I left Unisys. It was just in time because Kate started having problems with her jaw again. We got an appointment with Dr. Ryan and he said the artificial jaw joint he had installed years earlier had worn out. This was a problem because the FDA had stopped the use of them. So as a temporary fit he took one of Kate's ribs and shaped it as a jaw joint. In the mean time I wrote a letter to Congressman Dingle of Michigan who was on the FDA committee of my problem. I started working for Monroe Auto Equipment full time. The drive from Grand Rapids, Ohio to Monroe, Michigan was a long one especially in the winter. Mark who was still living with us graduated from Owens Community College, got a job, wanted to buy a house and moved out. Holly still had a little over a year left at Alma, But with Mark out on his own we were able to get a little money ahead. The Brittney Spaniel we brought with us from Pennsylvania passed away do to kidney problems.

The semester before Holly graduated she became a exchange student in Scotland at Kings College in the northern part of the country. Holly who played girls soccer at Alma became the only American on the Scottish College soccer team and kicked the winning goal in the championship. Needless to say we were quite proud of her. Holly met a young man while attending Alma, which was a pastor's son by the name of Joel Pestrue. He was also an exchange at Kings College, and their relationship grew. Both Holly and Joel graduated from Alma the following summer. Holly a chemistry major got a job at Upjohn Pharmaceuticals in Kalamazoo, Michigan, and Joel a Physiology major, got a job with the Michigan court system investing households where violence was taking place. They decided to move in together. With Joel's mother being a pastor, I was an elder in the church they were getting considerable heat from both sides. The following year Kate and I decided to move to Dundee, Michigan to be closer to the children and were I was working. Kate and I bought a double wide trailer in a trailer park in Dundee. We notified the children and they came in to help us to move. In the process of moving out of Grand Rapids, Ohio to Dundee the children notified us they were all getting married. Mark had met a good looking young lady from Athens, Greece, by the name of Angie, who lived across the street from where he bought a house in Toledo, Ohio. Mark and Angie were getting married in April the following year, and Holly and Joel were getting married in the following June.

Chapter Twelve

Our Move to Michigan

We moved to Dundee, Michigan and we started attending Dundee Presbyterian Church. Everything is going pretty well in our new home. We found a doctor in Monroe that we both liked that was just down the street from where I worked. We got a garden shed for all the ceramic molds that was even large enough for the pouring table. We were able to fire the kiln using the same outlet as the dryer, so we were back in business again working on ceramics for craft shows. Holly was going to Michigan State, working on her doctorate. She had gotten a scholarship for this from the federal government and the state. While going for her advanced degree she was to develop a way to reduce the toxins in the great lakes, which was starting to cause problems. Joel was still working for the Michigan court system. Things were to quite around the house without the kids, so for Kate birthday in November I took her to the human society in Monroe and we got a dog. Cinders was only a year old and was a German Shepard – Beagle mix. She had the markings of a Shepard but the size of a tall

Beagle. Cinders was definitely Kate's dog she followed her everywhere. In December before Christmas we were going back to Pennsylvania to see mom, who was in the Masonic Home. Mark and Angie came up to see us the evening before we left to go back to Pa. Angie noticed that Cinders tits were swollen, We did not think anything about it. A neighbor next door who had a Black German Shepard by the name of King, which liked to play with Cinders volunteered to look after Cinders while we were gone. The next morning we left early for Pennsylvania and leaving Cinder's in the care of the neighbor. We stayed with Pastor Ferguson and his wife at their home in Paradise, Pennsylvania. On Christmas Day after church we went to see mom at the Masonic Home. She enjoy seeing us and we had a nice visit.

However in Michigan, Cinder's gave birth to four puppies on Christmas day on my bed. The next door was beside himself and did not know what to do, so he called his mother in Kentucky. She told him not to worry Cinders would take care of everything and she did.

The day after Christmas Kate and I drove back to Michigan. It had snowed so I let Kate out while I cleaned out the driveway to park and unload. Cinders usually met us at the door, but that did not happen. Kate did not think anything of this Cinders was probably next door with King. I was unloading the car when Kate called. She walked into the bedroom and found Cinders nursing her four pups on my bed. Kate was using the room across from our bedroom as an art room. I pushed Kate's work table away from the doorway and went looking for a large box for Cinders a bed. Kate started to work on preparing dinner when Cinders came into the living room and got our attention she was going up and down the hall wanting us to follow her, which we did. One of the puppies had fallen of the bed on to the floor and she could not get it. We picked it up and put it on the bed with her and then she was happy. After dinner I fixed up a large box with paper shreds to be soft and put it in Kate's work room across from our bedroom. Cinders was very comfy in her bed with the puppies. Cinders was a very good mother. Every two hours she laid down with her puppies and fed them. However she would only allow Kate and I into Kate's work room, that room became hers with the puppies. Mark and Angie came up to see the puppies, but Cinders would only allow them in unless Kate or I was with them.

On Monday after the holiday I called the human society, because we were supposed to have Cinders spaded, which was not possible because she was nursing the pups. The human society asked me what the pups looked like and I said they were all different. One was black, one was all white, one was coco colored, and one was dark brown with the nose that looked like a boxer. They called Cinders a slut. I looked at Cinders who was sitting next to my leg and said they just called you a nasty name. It was shame because it was probably the first time she went into heat and was taken advantage of while running loose. We weaned the puppies and the Human society found them good homes. We had Cinders spaded and everything went back to normal.

A couple of years later the young man and his dog King moved away and sold his double wide to a lady with two teenage sons. It had been five years and Kate was starting to having problems with her jaw again. I communicated with Congressman Dingell again and he responded saying after five years the FDA had tentatively approved a new jaw joint and Kate was scheduled for one of these. I notified the insurance company and their response was that they would not pay for it since it was experimental. I started pricing out the cost to get a loan for it when the insurance company turned around their decision and said they would pay for it. It would take several trips to see Dr. Ryan before the surgery. The surgery required a 3D x-ray of Kate's head so a model of Kate's skull could be made to fit the new Titanium Joint before surgery.

The new neighbors moved in and we noticed after a short period of time a continual string of cars would come by I was concerned for Kate while I was at work. So on our trips out to Wisconsin to see Dr. Ryan we started to look for property to build what we hoped would be our retirement home. Kate was scheduled for surgery at the Medical College of Wisconsin, which was located in the Lutheran Hospital. The surgery took twelve hours and Dr. Ryan required an assistant. Kate came through the surgery ok, but the insurance company said they would not pay for the assistant surgeon. I called the insurance company up and asked if they could word twelve hours straight without help. The insurance company agreed to pay for the assistant. When everything was done and Kate came I still had part of the hospital bill to pay, which we agree on a payment plan of so much a month. It is interesting to note that the price before the insurance agreed to pay for the surgery was one third the price after the insurance agreed to pay. On our many trips out to Wisconsin to see Dr. Ryan before and after surgery we found a piece of property we could afford. It was located across the street from a lake called Loch Erin in the Irish Hills of Michigan, near the village of Onsted, Michigan. This was located about a half an hour west of where we were presently living. Holly received her doctorate from Michigan State, but continued to work there until Joel continued his education at Central Michigan University. Kate and I purchased the property on Loch Erin. Kate started having some respiratory problems, which we thought might be due to living just south of Dundee's cement plant. With the help of Mark and Angie we found a builder on Airport Highway not far from Toledo Express Airport. The builder agreed to purchase the double wide we were living in and move it to a foundation and sell it. He would build us a modular home with a two car garage and have a hobby room in between for the kiln and the railroad. The modular home would have a front porch the whole length of the front of the house. The Summer of 1998 the modular house was being built across the street from lake Loch Erin and we moved the fall of that year. I put the garden shed for the ceramic molds next to the garage. The kids gave us rocking chairs for Christmas so we could sit on the porch rock and watch the sun set over the lake. Kate continued to have respiratory problems and they were getting worse, The idea of it was due to the Dundee Cement plant proved to be wrong and we did not know what the problem was. We located a good doctor in Onsted so we had our medical records transferred from Dr. Miller in Monroe to Dr. VanSickel in Onsted instead of driving an hour to the doctors. I continued to work at Monroe Auto Equipment. The following summer I fenced in the back yard with Holly's help for Cinders to run. I also purchased a boat to go fishing in the lake, which I did about once a week. We lived on the south side of the lake, which was very cold in the winter. Cinders didn't even terry when I let her out the back door to potty. Cinder's enjoyed playing with the golden retriever next door. They enjoyed running up and down the fence together plowing snow with their noses. In the fall of the year 2000 my brother Solomon, his wife Mary, Kate, and I went together to Disney World. We spent five days in Disney World and four days on a Disney Cruise ship. We had a fantastic time.

We really enjoyed our home across the street from the lake but as I said Kate had respiratory problems, she was going to the hospital with bronchitis a lot and the only way Dr. VanSickel was able to control it was with steroids, which she kept increasing. I kept a medicine list of Kate's meds on the computer. One day when Kate was seeing the doctor I had left the medicine list in the truck. I had to go out to the truck to get it and I was winded when I got back. Dr. VanSickel asked me if that was normal. I said yes, but Dr. Miller said I just needed to lose some weight. She said that is something else and set me up to see a pulmonary doctor. He did a lot of tests and said the lower half of my lungs looked like concrete and asked where I worked with asbestos. My response was in the navy in 1964-5 at the radio station in Puerto Rico. I told my brother Solomon and he said I should apply for military disability since that is the only place I worked with asbestos. I applied filled out a lot of forms and had a lot more tests with more doctors. In the mean while Kate's health was getting worse. She started breaking vertebrae rolling over in bed because of the steroids. We saw a bone doctor at the University of Michigan Hospital. The doctor glued the vertebrae that he could get to with plastic, but he could not get to the ones that were not accessible from the back. Kate continued to have repertory problems and was in and out of the hospital and we could not figure out why.

I was still working at Monroe Auto Equipment calibrating industrial robots and I foreman of the calibration lab, which included quality being audited by Lloyds of London every year. They would check my records and spot checked the equipment. Everything was found in order for years, when Monroe Auto Equipment to decided to cut back. They laid off the co-ops that were helping me with all the calibration. This left me with a department of one, me. Failing an audit was not an option. I started working twelve hour days, six days a week getting ready for the next audit in a couple of weeks. I passed the audit, but left after the meeting listing the results. I was very sick. I went to Dr. VanSickel's office and I had a 104 temperature and my lungs were congested. She sent me to the pulmonary doctor. They sent me home to rest. This all happened September 9, 2001. I know this because the disaster in New York happened the 11th while I was still sick in bed. They met with me a few days later and told me that if I continued to work like this I would die next year. They even went as far to write to my boss and told him I needed help or else. Dying next year was not an option as far as I was concerned, I had a wife to take care of. Monroe Auto Equipment answer to all this was give me an early retirement. They gave me credit for ten years with the company and a lump sum big enough to hold us until I got social security. I was to train an engineer from another department until the end of the year. Retirement including a pension and health coverage. I was retired effective January 2, 2002. I had plenty to do around the house with the railroad, ceramics, and taking care of Kate. In 2004 mom died of heart failure at 93 while at the Masonic Home in Elizabethtown PA. We went back for the funeral. While we were back there we discussed Kate's health with Mary, who had been a nurse, and Solomon. We came to the conclusion that it may be the climate. Kate did not have these health problems in Pennsylvania before we moved north. It was colder and damper in Michigan. We went back to Michigan, but thinking about what we had discussed. I was able to get social security. To sublimit my income I was asked to help train people in two of their manufacturing plants how to calibrate their robots. Kate's health continued to get worse, when my claim for military disability came through. It took two and a half years to approve it and I thought it was a lost cause. As I said in the title of this book the Lord works in mysterious ways. It included a lump sum for the two and a half years I had to weight. Kate's health was the most important on my mind. Even though we loved our home across the street from the lake very much. Losing a wife was not an option. This wind fall of money gave us the ability to do something about it. We got up one morning and found Cinders dead laying under the dinning room table. That was a shock to us. She had been having some trouble with her back but other than that she had not been sick. We had her cremated and had her ashes put in a box. We put our house on the market and looked for a home we could afford in Pennsylvania. We found a double wide in Pheasant Ridge on the west side of Lancaster. We went back to Michigan and started to pack. Kate got very sick and ended up in the hospital.

Up to when I had gotten sick in September of 2001 we

had been attending a large Presbyterian Church in Brooklyn, Michigan. I missed church for over two weeks and no one missed us for over a year. We started attending a small Methodist Church in Springville, Michigan and became members and part of a church family. Something we did not feel in Brooklyn. It was the membership of the church in Springville that help me pack while Kate was in the hospital. I picked a low bid mover off the internet to move us. This was realized later to be a big mistake. The house was sold and the movers put everything in a truck headed for Pennsylvania. Kate was still in the hospital. I stayed at a motel until she was out of the hospital. It was a rainy day in early December 2004 when Kate got out of the hospital. I hooked up the boat behind the truck and we headed for Pennsylvania. We stayed at a motel until our furniture came. Mary had made a appointment with their doctor for Kate and he put her back in the hospital. This gave me time to have the roof replaced, which failed an inspection when the house was sold to us and the owner agreed to pay half, and have a ramp added at the back door since Kate was in a wheel chair. The moving company came with the furniture and the boxes. Solomon's daughter Kim helped me direct the movers since Kate was still in the hospital in Lancaster. Kate got home and out of the hospital the day after the roof and ramp was done. A few years before we left Michigan, Mark and Angie had a baby girl and called her Eva. Kate and I slowly got the furniture arranged the way we wanted it, but was had been put in boxes was pretty much smashed. It was obvious they had stacked boxes marked fragile in storage and that crushed what was inside. One piece I felt very bad about was an antique bowl and pitcher Kate's mother had given her was badly broke. I tried to glue it back together and Kate did not notice for a little while. When she did notice she was upset, but appreciated what I had try to do. I will never get a mover that is low bed off the internet again. The only things that were not broke were some special things such as the handmade grandfather's clock we had taken apart and wrapped well and put in the back of the pickup truck. When we looked at the house originally it had a garden shed in back. I did not put the shed in the sale agreement and when we moved in it was gone. I had to buy a shed to put the ceramic molds in. I ran electric to it so I could work out there after dark. We used the dryer outlet for the kiln. When we lived in Michigan we had the kids help us set up and tear down at craft shows. Back here in Pennsylvania it was just Kate and I and it became too much for us to do so eventually we gave it up. The health problems Kate had in Michigan slowly went away, which was the reason to move back to Pennsylvania.

Chapter Thirteen

Summary of our Life back in Pennsylvania

Kate and I finally got settled in to our home in Pheasant Ridge we got accounted with some nice neighbor across the street called Ed and Marie. Ed was a retired union machinery repairman at the Kellogg Cereal plant. Kate and I missed Cinders so we started stopping at the Human Society east of Lancaster on route 30 looking for a dog. On one of our stops we were about to leave, when they said there was a dog in a room that had been brought back and they were going to put him down. I looked in the room and did not see him at first. He was under a bench shacking. He had an overbite so bad his tong always hung out. The Human Society said his mother was a Jack Russell, she got out one day while in heat and this dog, which they called Dimples was the result. The father was unknown. They thought the dog had been spaded. We brought the home and he checked out every corner of the house. I told Kate that is not a Dimples, but a Snoopy. Snoopy was black, brown, white, with a long circled up tail. We took Snoopy to the same vet he went to as a puppy for a checkup, which was good we did because they said he had not been spaded, his testicles never dropped and that could cause cancer. We had Snoopy spaded so he would not get cancer. Snoopy was a little over a year old and was already house broke, however he would get me up at 6:00 am to go to the potty. That would become my schedule with Snoopy. After I took Snoopy to the potty and was dressed I would have coffee with Ed and we would solve the world's problems until Kate got up.

Holly's husband Joel finished his Physician's Assistant courses at Central Michigan University as well as his internship. They bought a house in East Tawas, Michigan that was next to where his mother lived, which was on the bank of Lake Huron. This is a great to visit and fish, but not a place to be in the winter time. Holly got a job as a professor teaching biology at Saginaw Valley University. Joel is a P.A. at a clinic not to far from where they live. They got a retriever and called her Alley. Alley loves swimming in the lake. After a couple of years Holly had a son and called him Jackson. Alley started sleeping under Jackson's crib and followed him everywhere. The house they bought was a summer home and was not insulated, which made it cold and drafty in the winter. Holly and Joel with the help of Ray, Joel's step father started building a two car garage with a apartment above it. They moved in before the following winter.

Mark got his engineering degree from the University of Toledo, which is where Angie received her office management degree. Mark is now the Chief Engineer for an Engineering Company not too far from where they moved to in Springfield Township, which is west of Toledo. They have a very nice two story house, which Mark has done a lot of work to. Kate and I visit Mark, Angie, and Eva in the summer.

In the summer of 2008 Kate had a bad stroke and I almost lost her. I was having some troubles cutting the grass because of my lung problem slowing getting worse. After Kate recovered and was home after the stroke, Mark and Holly said we needed to make a life style change and they would help us do it. Holly gave us a list of retirement homes to look in around Lancaster County. Kate and I had been looking to see what was available before, but not in earnest. We looked at the ones on Holly's list and we either did not like them or they cost too much. A place called Lancashire Terrace was on Holly's list. We did not know where it was so Kate called. They said they were having an open house the next day which included lunch and gave us directions to come. We liked what we saw, which was cottages which they maintained and it was affordable. We put our double wide on the market. In 2009 it sold, but not without a lot of grief. We went back up to Lancashire Terrace and signed an agreement and made a deposit. Management at the terrace was to take a one bedroom cottage and add another bedroom for the railroad with a half a bath, fence in the back yard for Snoopy. And add a deck. By July 2009 we were able to move in. The cottage has a kitchenette and a dining room / living room. There is a washer/dryer combination in the master bath room along and a shower. We go to a dining hall at five in the evening and have a brunch every other Friday. Ed and Marie and family helped us move in.

Kate and I tried to down size before we moved in but not enough. This is small but we like it and we are comfortable.

Holly, Joel, and Jackson moved into their apartment and Holly and a second son by the name of Liam. There is five years between the two boys but they get along well. In the summer as I mentioned before Kate and I go out to see the children and grandchildren. We don't drive it in one day any more. We leave on a Thursday and drive as far as Pittsburg and spend the night. The next day we go on to Mark and Angie's house. We spend the weekend there and then on Monday we drive north to Holly and Joel's house near East Tawas. The day after Christmas, Holly and family go to Mark's and the day after that they all drive down here to Pennsylvania. That way we get to see them twice a year.

2014 was not a good year. The VA thought I really did not have a lung condition as bad as I did and would be still alive. That summer they had me go through all the testing all over again, which took more than an week. After it was all over they apologized for thinking I was faking it and continued my hundred present disability. That same year Snoopy developed diabetes and within a month she went blind. Kate and I did not move any furniture around and we kept her food and water dishes in the same place so she got around ok even though she was blind. I gave her insulin shots twice a day at the same times. Snoopy know when they were due and even came up to me for her shot. The next year she started crying when she had to potty and I had to help her outside. Kate and I figured that Snoop's quality of life had become poor and decided to have her put to sleep. We had Snoopy cremated and her and Cinder's reside in boxes under the white Rose of Sharyn in the front of the cottage.

In December of 2015 Kate had a minor stroke which put her in the hospital. She was confused for a while but that cleared up, however her right vocal cord stopped working and this never did fully recover. Kate has to eat slowly to keep from chocking. In 2016 Kate and I went to Disney World by train and stayed in the Animal Kingdom for our 50th Wedding Anniversary. We had a great time.

Well Kate and I are in our seventies and living fairly well in Lancashire Terrace. When we lived in Pheasant Ridge we attended church regularly at Donegal Presbyterian Church where I was a deacon. With our move to the Terrace, which is north of the city of Lancaster in Neffsville, it was too far to travel to Donegal. We have not found a small church where we feel comfortable. We do however attend the religious sing-alongs with Grace who is a Baptist Pastor. We attend St. Peter's Lutheran Church periodically, but we will always be Presbyterians. Kate and I visit Pastor Ferguson who now retired and lives at the Ware Presbyterian Village in Oxford. He was our pastor for thirty years and we still stay in touch. Well I guess I have rambled on long enough and you probably find this boring so I am closing.

NRS/SS:RC:srw
14-66
29 March 1966

From: Chaplain, U. S. Naval Radio Station (R) Sabana Seca
To: LITTLE, Richard R., Jr., 596-55-81, ETN2, USNR
Via: Commanding Officer, U. S. Naval Reserve Unit, Folsom, Pennsylvania

Subj: Letter of Appreciation

1. As Chairman of the Boy Scout Committee, I wish to express, to you, the appreciation of the entire command for your untiring efforts in behalf of the boys at this station. Troop 170 and the U. S. Naval Radio Station (R) Sabana Seca hold it a privilege to have served with you.

2. Your further efforts in behalf of the Protestant Chapel Choir are also recognized and commended.

3. Your contribution to the life of the Station in fostering better morale and in the social and religious life of the men is in the highest traditions of the Navy. Well done.

4. It is recommended that a copy of this letter be made a part of your permanent service record.

Robert J. Edwards

Robert J. EDWARDS
LT, CHC, USNR

- -

QR/WRO:clm
13 April 1966

FIRST ENDORSEMENT

From: Commanding Officer, NRSD 4-62(M), Folsom, Pa.
To: LITTLE, Richard R., Jr., 596 55 81, ETN2, USNR-R

1. Forwarded. Your work at prior duty station, assures me of your ability to do a fine job for us.

W R O'Gara

W. R. O'GARA

Printed in the United States
By Bookmasters